WHAAM!

THE ART & LIFE OF

ROY LICHTENSTEIN

Susan Goldman Rubin

ABRAMS BOOKS FOR YOUNG READERS • NEW YORK

LOOK MICKEY, 1961.

One day in 1961 Roy Lichtenstein had a crazy idea for a painting. Why not use comic book characters for his subjects? He was inspired by an illustration in a Little Golden Book, Walt Disney's *Donald Duck Lost and Found*. Roy enlarged and simplified the picture, and changed the color and composition. But he kept the joke. Donald Duck thinks he has caught a fish, but he has really hooked the back of his own jacket.

Another story relates that Roy's young son David came home from school and said that the teacher had asked the pupils to tell what their fathers did for a living. David complained that all the other fathers had interesting jobs. "And you're an artist and you can't draw," he said to Roy.

Supposedly Roy took out a canvas and sketched the figures of Donald Duck and Mickey Mouse. It led to his breakthrough painting, *Look Mickey*.

"When I put *Look Mickey* next to my abstractions, I just could never go back to the abstractions," said Roy.

Almost overnight Roy became a leading figure in the new movement called Pop Art. No one was more surprised at his enormous success than he was.

For an artist known for outrageous paintings, Roy had a normal, uneventful childhood. He was born on October 27, 1923. His mother once commented that he never got into trouble and was always polite and well behaved.

Roy grew up in New York City and went to public school until he was twelve. He liked to draw and had an easel in his bedroom. "His friends always wandered in and watched him paint," recalled his younger sister, Renée. They also liked to watch him make model airplanes and invent different kinds of machines. Roy became fascinated with science one year when he got a chemistry set as a Christmas present. For a while he thought he would be a scientist when he grew up.

The Lichtensteins were Jewish but nonpracticing, which was not uncommon in Germany, where Roy's grandparents had come from. They celebrated Jewish holidays like Passover as well as Christmas. Roy and Renée's father, Milton, was a real estate broker who managed garages and parking lots. Their mother, Beatrice, stayed at home taking care of the family, including her father, who lived with them. Roy's middle name, Fox, came from his great-grandfather on his mother's side.

The Lichtensteins had a comfortable apartment on West Eighty-sixth Street. In those days, before there was TV, Roy and Renée used to lie on their stomachs on the living room floor and listen to the radio. Roy's favorite programs were *Flash Gordon*, based on a science fiction comic book character, and *Buck Rogers in the 25th Century*, which followed the adventures of the earliest space hero and his friendly scientist-inventor assistant. Hearing those shows may have inspired Roy's sci-fi comic book paintings, such as *Mad Scientist*.

MAD SCIENTIST, 1963.

Their apartment was near the American Museum of Natural History. Often Roy walked there by himself and wandered through the halls lined with life-size dioramas. The Hall of Northwest Coast Indians especially intrigued him. On outings to the Museum of Modern Art, Roy took his sister along. "He explained everything to me," she remembered. Most of all he admired the art of Pablo Picasso and Paul Klee, and these artists were to have a lasting influence on his work.

During the summers Roy went to camp and played sports, but without much enthusiasm. "I was good at swimming," he recalled. A photo of him in his bathing trunks shows him proudly flexing his biceps to prove his strength. Around this time he heard blues on the radio and became excited about jazz. Back in New York, he went to Carnegie Hall with his friend Don Wolf to hear Benny Goodman perform and briefly took up the clarinet himself.

In 1936, when he was thirteen, Roy entered the eighth grade at Franklin School for Boys, a private school. There were no art lessons there, so he started taking watercolor classes every Saturday morning at Parsons School of Design. By the time he was fifteen, he knew he wanted to be an artist instead of a scientist. Despite so-so grades, he finished four years of high school in three. "His projects interested him more than schoolwork," said Renée.

The summer after he graduated, Roy attended a painting class at the Art Students League. His teacher, Reginald Marsh, was famous for his paintings of New York crowd scenes. Marsh came to class only fifteen minutes a week, and Roy and the other students hardly ever saw him. Yet Roy loved the class. For the first time he painted directly from a live model and studied anatomical drawing. He observed the person posing from different points of view as he tried to understand the structure of the human body, the relationship between bones and muscles, and proportion—the relative sizes of hands and feet, eyes and head. Roy wanted to stay at the League or take classes at some other New York art school instead of going to college. Although his parents approved of his goal to be an artist, they worried about how he would earn a living. They urged him to go to college and get a liberal arts degree that would qualify him to teach. So Roy applied to Ohio State University, College of Education, which included the School of Fine and Applied Arts, and he was accepted.

In autumn of 1940, just before his seventeenth birthday, Roy went to Columbus, Ohio, and began his studies.

ABOVE: SENIOR PHOTO OF ROY, 1940, FRANKLIN HIGH SCHOOL YEARBOOK.

OPPOSITE: ROY, AGE TEN, LAKE BUEL, MA.

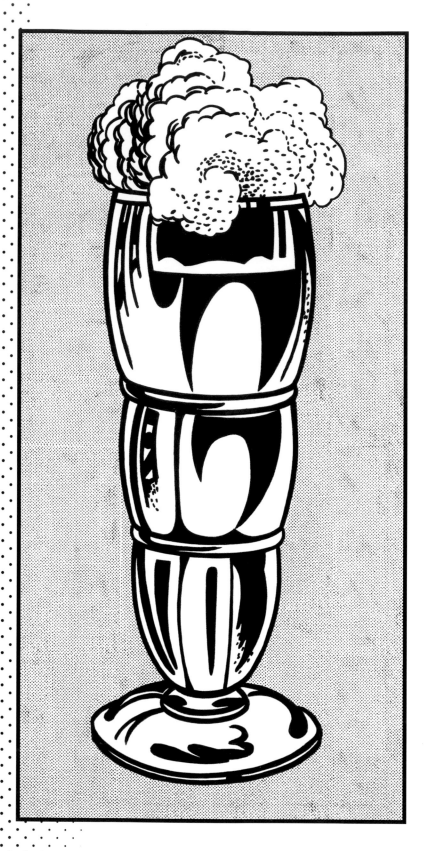

"I had no idea what art was then," he recalled. "I was very foggy about the whole thing."

The professor who influenced him most was Hoyt Sherman. "He taught me how to go about learning how to look," said Roy. Hoyt, an engineer as well as an artist and art professor, developed a program of "flash labs." In a darkened room, he briefly flashed slides on a screen for a split second. Then the students had to draw what they had seen. "The images became progressively more complex," said Roy. Next Sherman presented the students with a single three-dimensional object dangling from a rope—familiar things like a chair, a wastebasket, or a can. The idea was to observe closely. "If a person looks attentively at an object without moving his eyes," said Sherman, "he will see it as a perceptual unit." That is, something that can be immediately recognized and understood. Sherman believed this method would increase anyone's powers of observation, and he taught dental students and football players in addition to artists. Roy said that this program "became the center of what I was interested in. I'd always wanted to know the difference between a mark that was art and one that wasn't."

ICE CREAM SODA, 1962.

Sherman also talked about size. In children's art, the larger the size, the greater the significance of the subject. Roy later thought of this when he created paintings of larger-than-life single objects: an ice-cream soda, a hot dog, a ball of twine.

Halfway through his junior year in college, he was drafted into the army to serve in World War II. Roy's diverse training included basic engineering, preliminary pilot and navigator classes, and work as a draftsman and artist for combat plans. By December 1944, soldiers were needed overseas, and Roy shipped out with an engineer battalion and served in England, France, Belgium, and Germany. Looking back, he didn't feel as though he had been in any danger. "We were winning the war quite easily at that point," he said.

When World War II ended in Europe in May 1945, Roy's unit stayed overseas as a policing force. While stationed in Paris, he enrolled at the Cité Internationale Universitaire to study French and civilization. In letters to his family he wrote that he enjoyed visiting art museums and buying art books. But soon he was called home on furlough because his father was very sick. In January 1946, Roy's father died. Later that month Roy was discharged from the army, after serving for three years. Fulfilling his parents' wishes, he returned to Ohio State University to continue his studies and graduated in June.

Roy was asked to teach at Ohio State, and he accepted in September 1946. That autumn, he enrolled in the master of fine arts program with Hoyt Sherman as his adviser.

Paying tribute to his artistic heroes, he wrote in his thesis,

In awe, then, you must sing,
An Ode to the Wonderful Wizards of Art,
Sing of Klee's secret glee,
And of Picasso's electric expression.

In 1949 he received his master of fine arts degree and soon afterward married Isabel Wilson, an assistant in an artists' cooperative gallery in Cleveland. While Roy

continued to teach at Ohio State, he began a series of paintings that featured fairy tales and medieval-history subjects. In a whimsical self-portrait he pictured himself as a smiling medieval knight. At that time his style was consciously childlike, similar to Paul Klee's. Roy exhibited his work in the Midwest and even had an early solo show in New York City, followed by numerous others.

His teaching position at Ohio State ended in 1951, and he and his wife moved to Cleveland. To earn money he did a variety of jobs, from decorating department store windows to designing products for a steel corporation. Every six months he'd take time off to devote to art. "I was painting cowboys and Indians then, historical things," he said. "I was taking the kind of stodgy pictures you see in history textbooks and redoing them in a modern way." Roy's paintings on Native American Indian themes perhaps came from memories of the feathered bird masks and totem poles he had seen as a boy at the American Museum of Natural History.

In 1954 his son David Hoyt was born and named for Roy's professor. Another son, Mitchell Wilson, was born in 1956. With a growing family to support, Roy needed a steady income, so he decided to go back to teaching. In 1957 the State University of

INDIAN PADDLING A
CANOE, 1956.

New York Teachers College at Oswego offered him an assistant professorship and he took it. During this period Roy again changed his way of painting and began to work in an Abstract Expressionist style with stripes and squiggles of bright color.

By 1958, somehow, cartoon characters sneaked into his pictures. "I began putting hidden comic images into those paintings, such as Mickey Mouse, Donald Duck, and Bugs Bunny," he said. These odd paintings startled Roy and he was afraid to show them to anybody. What would people think? At that time comic books were not appreciated as anything but light entertainment. They had become popular after World War II but were considered "lowbrow" and vulgar compared to book art and fine art in museums. Art schools would never encourage students to use such dreadful, crass material as subject matter.

In the spring of 1960 Roy was invited to teach at Douglass College, the women's college of Rutgers University in New Jersey, and he accepted.

One of his best new friends was Allan Kaprow, an art history teacher at Rutgers as well as a daring, experimental artist who created "environments" out of such things as a pile of tires. This was a new kind of art, unlike traditional paintings or sculptures. Kaprow also produced unusual theatrical events called "Happenings," in which artist-performers did presentations like sitting in chicken coops rattling noisemakers, and painting one canvas collectively. Roy had great fun attending the shows and they loosened him up. The Happenings, he said, were "the greatest influence on my work . . . Kaprow made it clear to me that my work did not have to look like art . . . I wanted to say something that hadn't been said before." And Roy's teacher Hoyt Sherman had urged art students to "create fresh, new designs."

Roy's big breakthrough came in the summer of 1961 when he was thirty-seven years old. Kaprow had come to visit with his family. While their wives and kids were out shopping, Kaprow and Roy discussed how to teach students about color. Roy explained that he was having his students look at the paintings of Paul Cézanne (one of his favorite artists), who used graduated colors to compose the relationship of a figure to its background, such as with dark colors in the middle of a light area or the reverse. When the kids came back, they had a bag full of Dubble Bubble gum, the kind with comics printed on the wrappers. Kaprow pulled out one of the cartoons, laid it out flat, and said to Roy, "You can't teach color from Cézanne, you can only teach it from something like this."

MADAME CÉZANNE IN THE CONSERVATORY, 1891, BY PAUL CÉZANNE.

POPEYE, 1961.

"He looked at me with the funniest grin on his face," remembered Kaprow. "Come with me," said Roy. Kaprow followed him up to his studio, which was on the second floor of the house. "He lifted up a lot of abstract canvases that were tacked to the wall and showed me the one at the back, which was an abstract painting with Donald Duck in it." For a moment Kaprow stood there, puzzled. Then he let out a huge laugh.

Roy felt encouraged. That summer he began to paint big cartoon paintings. One of the first, *Look Mickey*, was a greatly enlarged version based on the illustration by Bob Grant and Bob Totten in a Little Golden Book. With a pencil Roy drew the outlines freehand onto the canvas, then he painted in the areas with flat primary colors: red, yellow, and blue. "I got some of these colors from supermarket packaging," said Roy. "I would look at package labels to see what colors had the most impact on one another." He took a few words of the text by Carl Buettner and put them into a word bubble as part of the composition.

MAGNIFYING GLASS, 1963.

Next came *Popeye*, complete with "force lines" to express physical power, just like in the comics. Some people thought that Popeye represented Roy—feisty, and though slightly built (compared to his opponent Bluto), strong enough to deliver the knockout punch.

Roy wanted his paintings to look like mechanical reproductions produced by printing methods instead of hand-painted images. To achieve this effect he copied the newspaper process invented by Benjamin Day, an American illustrator, of printing shades of color with tiny dots. Only Roy did not print the dots but painted each one. He enlarged the Benday dots to make them clearly visible. "I'm not using commercial techniques," he once explained. "I'm *simulating* commercial techniques." His humorous black-and-white painting *Magnifying Glass* lets the viewer in on the secret. Through the

magnifying glass one sees what those little printed dots look like when they're blown up. (Except that Roy had actually painted them!) The first time he used Benday dots, he applied them with a dog-grooming brush dipped in oil paint. Then he made his own metal stencils with dots of varying sizes and rubbed the paint through the holes with a toothbrush.

He branched out from cartoons and comic strip panels to printed advertisements for his ideas. Going through newspapers, magazines, and the yellow pages of the phone book, he clipped images and pasted them into his composition notebooks. *Girl with Ball*, for instance, was based on an ad that he saw in the *New York Times* for a resort in the Pocono Mountains. *Ice Cream Soda* came from the menu of a diner in New Jersey. An ad for a sneaker resulted in *Keds*. Roy even began a series of mural-size paintings of the black-and-white speckled covers of his composition notebooks. "What I did in these early paintings in 1961 was frightening to me," said Roy. "Everything was counter to what I had

TOP: KEDS, 1962.

BOTTOM: PAGE FROM JERICHO COMPOSITIONS NOTEBOOK WITH AD IN COLOR FOR A SNEAKER, ALSO ADS CLIPPED FOR T-SHIRT, TELEPHONE, ALARM CLOCK, ETC.

OPPOSITE: GIRL WITH BALL, 1962.

both been taught and really appreciated." Unlike the paintings of the masters he admired such as Paul Cézanne, who had an atmospheric feeling for nature and portrayed forms with subtle tones of color, Roy's work, in his own words, had "no humanity." His pictures of a waste can and a ball of twine were intentionally mechanical. "But very shortly," he said, "I knew that it had more meaning than the things I had done before."

His friend Kaprow arranged for him to bring his exciting work to the prestigious Leo Castelli Gallery in New York City, which specialized in modern art. Roy had been there before on his own with his abstract stripe paintings, but the dealer had not been interested. However, Castelli liked the new work, and a few weeks later he decided to give Roy a one-person show. Around this time another young artist brought his cartoon and comic book paintings to Castelli. His name was Andy Warhol.

Warhol based his paintings on the comics he had enjoyed as a child: *Nancy*, *Dick Tracy*, and *Popeye*. Roy, on the other hand, was inspired by movies, cartoons, comics, advertisements, illustrations, and art reproductions of all types. Since Warhol's work was similar to Roy's, Castelli turned it down. But Roy and Warhol became friends. By coincidence they were both using advertising and popular culture as subjects but in totally different ways. Warhol came from a background in commercial art and had illustrated advertisements printed in newspapers and magazines. In his painting he and his assistants utilized silk screens to mass-produce his pictures. Roy, a studio painter and college instructor, *mimicked* the mechanical perfection of the printing process. He didn't create his work in mass but one at a time, almost always by and for himself. Comic books, Roy said, offered great "possibilities for paintings." He liked the challenge of making art out of "non-art."

At that time other artists were also turning to comics and advertisements for inspiration. Ed Ruscha painted *OOF* and *OK* with just the comic book words. Claes Oldenburg, a member of the Happenings group, did a version of Mickey Mouse, and Robert Rauschenberg put actual pieces of newspaper onto his paintings. Like Roy, these modern artists were taking the lowest symbols of American culture as immediately recognizable subject matter in order to grab people's attention with familiar images. They wanted to enliven fine art and make it more accessible. Why take everything so seriously like the Abstract Expressionists such as Franz Kline and Willem de Kooning? Or Jackson Pollock, who, in 1950, painted *Autumn Rhythm (Number 30)*, a canvas more than eighteen feet long layered with drips, swirls, and spatters?

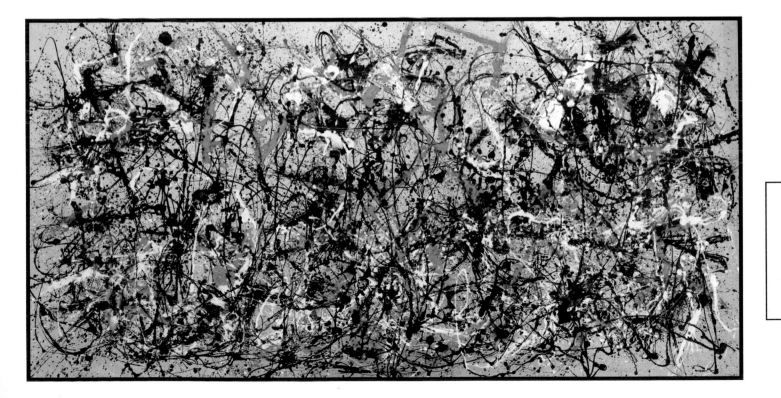

AUTUMN RHYTHM (NUMBER 30), 1950, BY JACKSON POLLOCK.

Critics soon linked Roy and his peers as Pop Artists although they were doing different things. "Food always plays some sort of a part in Pop," said Roy. He made cartoon paintings of prepared foods such as *Turkey* and *Cherry Pie*, whereas Warhol created pictures of packages—Campbell's soup cans and Coca-Cola bottles. Oldenburg sculpted a larger-than-life soft vinyl hamburger, and Wayne Thiebaud painted pictures of gum-ball machines and pieces of pie. One critic wrote, "I am annoyed to have to see in a gallery what I'm forced to look at in a supermarket."

Not surprisingly, when it came time for Roy's first solo show to open at the Leo Castelli Gallery in February 1962, he felt "apprehensive." How would his work be received? Would people like his wacky new pictures? To his amazement the paintings sold out before opening night. Architect Philip Johnson bought *Girl with Ball* and later gave it to the Museum of Modern Art. Other important collectors bought *Turkey* and *Blam!*, a painting based on World War II comics. *Blam!* shows a plane that has just been hit and has flipped over as it breaks apart. *Whaam!* portrays a fighter pilot hitting an enemy aircraft with an explosive blast. Through the centuries war had always been a major theme for artists. Roy, however, used comic book war stories as source material to exaggerate clichés, or idealized stereotypes about World War II. In *Whaam!* the American pilot is a caricature of the good guy who fearlessly destroys the enemy in a blaze of glory.

Although Roy modeled his war paintings on comic strips, he made many changes as he designed his compositions. "My work is actually different from comic strips in that every mark is really in a different place, however slight the difference seems to some," he once said. "All the colors are different, all of the weights of line, the texture is different . . . nothing is the same." He enlarged the small images to huge proportions. *Whaam!*, for instance, gives the winning plane and the enemy plane equal importance in two enormous panels, each 68 by 83 inches. Much of his early Pop Art was to be based on other printed art illustrations.

Many people hated his solo show. Conventional critics were shocked. Angry. Horrified. Some claimed that Roy was not an artist at all! Twentieth-century "fine" artists painted serious pictures, not "dumb" images from comics and ads. Reviewers described his work as "jokey" and "empty-headed." They thought he was merely copying comic books for the same mass audience that read them, mainly children. Even the comic book artists criticized Roy's paintings as too flat and stylized compared to their own work. "Pop Artists or Copy Cats?" asked a journalist in the title of his review. A critic in *The New York Times* wrote that Roy was "one of the worst artists in the world." In response an article in *Life* magazine asked, "Is he the worst artist in the U.S.?" The reporter, Dorothy Seiberling, said, "For some of America's best-known critics and a host of laymen, the answer . . . is a resounding YES." She went on to note how Roy started as an artist and how he made his paintings. But ultimately she asked: "But is it art?"

BLAM!, 1962.

WHAAM!, 1963.

PANEL FROM "STAR JOCKEY," IN *ALL AMERICAN MEN OF WAR*, NO. 89 (JANUARY—FEBRUARY 1962), D.C. COMICS, BY IRV NOVICK.

The question "What is art?" had long concerned Roy. He said, "I had always wanted to know the difference between a mark that was art and one that wasn't." Half jokingly he answered the question in his painting *Art* by spelling out the letters A-R-T in white and red against a gold-colored background. A collector could hang it on his wall and proudly point to it saying, "This is art."

Over the next two years, despite the controversy stirred up by his work (or perhaps because of it), Roy became famous as a Pop Art painter. Critics, ordinary viewers, and artists themselves began to accept and appreciate his work and to recognize the originality of his Benday dots. He had his first group show in Amsterdam, and solo shows in Los Angeles and Pasadena, California, and exhibited works throughout the United States. In his painting *Masterpiece*, based on a comic book, he makes fun of his own success. And it was true. Collectors and museums paid higher and higher prices for Roy's art. Castelli continued to handle his work and remained his primary dealer for the rest of his life. "My dream has come true," Roy said to a friend. "I can't believe it." To another friend he said, "I wonder how long it's going to last." By 1963 Roy was earning enough money from the sales of his artwork to give up teaching and paint full time.

MASTERPIECE, 1962.

WE ROSE UP SLOWLY ...AS IF WE DIDN'T BELONG TO THE OUTSIDE WORLD ANY LONGER ...LIKE SWIMMERS IN A SHADOWY DREAM ... WHO DIDN'T NEED TO BREATHE...

ROY LICHTENSTEIN WITH HIS SONS, DAVID AND MITCHELL, IN HIS STUDIO, 1964, WITH *WE ROSE UP SLOWLY*, 1964, IN THE BACKGROUND.

There were changes in his personal life, too. He and his wife separated in 1963; they divorced in 1967. Roy moved to New York but stayed close to his sons, who lived with their mother in New Jersey, near Princeton. The boys split their time between their parents. A photo shows young David and Mitchell sprawled on the floor of their dad's studio reading comics from his collection while he works on the 92-inch-high painting *We Rose Up Slowly*. The painting depicts a man and woman underwater as they are about to kiss. It is based on a panel from "Sincerely Yours," a story in the comic *Girls' Romances*.

Roy turned to romance comic books aimed at teenagers for source material during this period. But he stayed away from famous comic book artists whose work was easily recognizable. Nevertheless, some comic book artists were amazed and even angry to find their work imitated by a fine artist. One threatened to sue Roy but didn't. William Overgard realized that Roy's painting *I Can See the Whole Room . . . And There's Nobody in It!* was very similar to the last panel of his *Steve Roper* comic. But, contrarily, Overgard took it as a compliment. He wrote a letter to *Time* magazine in response to its article blasting an exhibit of Pop Art at the Guggenheim Museum in New York. *Time* printed the letter with reproductions of the painting and the comic book panel. "Very flattering . . . I think?" wrote Overgard.

For Roy the subject was a joke on the theme of seeing. The man in his painting flips aside the cover of a peephole and peers into a space that is entirely black. Is he looking at the artist or the viewer? Who is watching whom? In another painting, *Image Duplicator*, a pair of threatening, grotesque eyes stare out with the word bubble, "**WHAT?** WHY DID YOU ASK ABOUT **THAT?** WHAT DO YOU KNOW ABOUT MY **IMAGE DUPLICATOR**?" It was as though Roy were challenging anyone who questioned his process.

Most of the comic book artists realized that Roy changed their images as he composed his paintings. The most obvious difference was size, but it was also their intention that differed.

TOP: *I CAN SEE THE WHOLE ROOM . . . AND THERE'S NOBODY IN IT!*, 1961.

RIGHT: COMIC BOOK PANEL FROM *STEVE ROPER*, AUGUST 6, 1961, BY WILLIAM OVERGARD.

Drowning Girl, for instance, comes from a panel in "Run for Love!" a story in a DC comic book. Roy's enormous version measures 67 ⅝ by 66 ¾ inches. He left out many of the words, including the title, and shortened the girl's word bubble. In Roy's painting she says tearfully, "I DON'T CARE! I'D RATHER SINK—THAN CALL BRAD FOR HELP!" In the original comic the boy's name is Mal and he's clinging to an overturned boat in the background. Roy left him out of the picture too. And he never let the viewer know whether or not she drowned. The story didn't matter. And the words were merely part of the design. "I really think of the lettering as a pattern of gray and the shape of a balloon as any other shape," he said.

Larger-than-life heads of crying girls became a repeated theme in Roy's paintings. Various panels of tearful girls clipped from comics filled his notebook, but he developed only a few of these into paintings. When he did, he began by drawing. "Most of my thinking really occurs on the drawing," he said. "I try to get it worked out as much as possible." With an opaque projector Roy magnified and transferred his drawing onto a canvas, often as large as nine feet by nine feet. The projector sat on a table and Roy put the drawing under the top lid. When the image was thrown on the canvas, Roy went up close and drew and erased and redrew the outlines of the shapes. "Once I am involved with the painting," he said, "I think of it as an abstraction. Half the time they are upside down anyway, when I work." He invented a special kind of easel system that ran the length of his studio wall. At any point slats could go higher or lower, and adjust to hold a canvas that was horizontal or vertical, and even tilt sideways. And he had freestanding easels that rotated in a full circle.

Sometimes he looked at the painting in a mirror to see it reversed. "When you suddenly look at it in a mirror, the things that are wrong to you seem to be more emphasized," he said. "You're seeing the image over again as though you're seeing it for the first time."

Roy worked on many paintings at once, lining them up side by side along his easel scaffolding with more drawings taped to the wall above.

The glamorous beauties in his paintings of girls came to life one day in 1964 when he met Dorothy Herzka at a New York art gallery where she worked. They married in

DROWNING GIRL, 1963.

1968, and though she never posed for him, friends noticed her uncanny resemblance to the gorgeous young women in Roy's comic book paintings.

"I did as many different things as I could," he said, "products and objects and girls and war . . . I worked on a variety because there were so many things to do at that time."

GRRRRRRRRRR!!, 1965.

His painting *Grrrrrrrrrr!!* was modeled after a K-9 marine dog named Pooch who starred in the DC comic *Our Fighting Forces*. Pooch fought World War II battles in the South Pacific with his buddies Gunner and Sarge. *Grrrrrrrrrr!!* portrays Pooch facing down his enemy. He looks menacing: head lowered, ears up, muscles taut, growling. Is the enemy really Roy's critics?

Pooch may have appealed to Roy because he and his family loved dogs. In Cleveland they had a German shepherd. Later, in Southampton, in addition to a black Lab named Spot, they adopted Fred, a neighbor's stray mix. They also had a marmalade cat named Louie. When Roy's son Mitchell went away to college, they took in Camille, Mitchell's collie.

Around the mid-1960s, Roy started painting something different: landscapes. Nature has been a traditional subject for artists through the centuries. Roy used his unique style of Benday dots, black outlines, and flat primary colors to create cliché sunrises and sunsets. Sometimes he saw a photo that inspired him, but mostly he invented the pictures. In his notebooks he played with ideas for compositions. Drawings in colored pencil of *Setting Sun and Sea* and the sun sinking behind hills filled the pages. He developed *Sinking Sun* into a huge painting, composed of layers of horizontal shapes topped off with stylized or exaggerated rays of white sunlight beaming from a bank of clouds.

SINKING SUN, 1964.

DRAWINGS FOR *SETTING SUN AND SEA* AND *HOT DOG*, 1964. ON LINED PAPER IN NOTEBOOK.

ABOVE: *HEAD WITH BLUE SHADOW, 1965.*

OPPOSITE: *BRUSHSTROKES, 1965.*

In 1964 Roy also turned to sculpture. Throughout his life he had enjoyed making things. Now he bought some mannequin heads of girls, added plaster, cast them in ceramic, and painted the hair and faces in dots, black lines, and solid blues, reds, and yellows. *Head with Blue Shadow*, for example, resembles a pretty girl with red dots on one side of her face and neck, and blue dots on the other. He told a museum curator, "I've always wanted to make up someone as a cartoon. That's what led to my ceramic sculptures of girls . . . I was going to make up a model with black lines around her lips, dots on her face and a yellow dyed wig with black lines drawn on it . . . I was interested in putting two-dimensional symbols on a three-dimensional object." Roy would continue to translate two-dimensional subjects into sculptures during his career, always starting with drawings.

In 1965 he began a new series of paintings. Each canvas features an enormously exaggerated brushstroke. "The starting point of the brushstroke thing was something I ran across in a comic book," he said. The comic book was called *Strange Suspense Stories*.

"Although I had played with the idea before," said Roy, "it started with a comic book image of a mad artist crossing out, with a large brush stroke 'X,' the face of a fiend that was haunting him . . . The painting included the brush stroke 'X,' the brush, and the artist's hand." The man in the comic book stands before the dripping strokes he's just painted and thinks, "I must be having some kind of nightmare."

Not Roy. He was having fun. In his version, four feet by four feet, he left out the words and redesigned the "X" as horizontal brushstrokes overlapping vertical ones. People in the art world knew that Roy was referring to the Abstract Expressionists who took their swirls and

splatters of paint so seriously and perhaps even to his own earlier brushstroke abstract paintings. Roy admitted in an interview, "The brush strokes obviously refer to Abstract Expressionism." Whereas those artists randomly created many brushstrokes, Roy carefully composed just one or two in each picture. "I thought brushstrokes kind of symbolize painting," he said. "Of course, they're cartoons of brushstrokes, so they're very unlike real brushstrokes." Laughing, he said, "Even in the beginning they looked to me like bacon or something."

Some years later he thought of translating works from the Brushstrokes series into enormous aluminum sculptures. "It was just some idea I got in the middle of the night," he said. "The fact that you would try to make a brushstroke out of some other material is bizarre. It seemed like an interesting thing to do because every sculpture would be a salute to painting in a certain way."

TOKYO BRUSHSTROKE II, 1994.

An architectural firm in Tokyo, Japan, commissioned him to create an outdoor sculpture for the front of its office building. In his studio, Roy began the project by playing with painted shapes of paper Brushstrokes left over from paper collages he had made. As he stood the pieces up at angles from one another, he got an idea. "I think I'm going to draw around it," he said. Next he cut foam board into shapes like the paper ones to make a scale model. Then, on paper taped to the wall, he drew the shapes in their actual size, thirty feet high, so that the pattern could be copied exactly in aluminum by the fabricators at a foundry. On the day of the unveiling, Roy climbed up a ladder and dusted off the top parts of *Tokyo Brushstrokes*. He was thrilled. "I felt victorious that we had carried this out from a drawing to an actual installation of the sculpture," he said. "Sort of amazing!"

With his playful sense of humor Roy painted a series in the late sixties showing what the *back* of his canvas might look like. Once again he took a common object, something in his studio, and made a painting of it. Artists usually stapled the canvas to a wooden frame to keep it from buckling. *Stretcher Frame with Cross Bars III* depicts the wooden frame and corner wedges holding the canvas taut. A viewer might wonder, Is this the real painting?

and perhaps feel tempted to turn it around. Roy said that he wanted to show people "something they haven't seen." (And also something they couldn't see: the "front.") He did the Stretcher Frame series in a limited palette of yellow, black, and white with his signature Benday dots and diagonal lines. In *Stretcher Frame Revealed Beneath Painting of a Stretcher Frame*, Roy takes the theme one step further. The painting of the back of the canvas looks as though it's peeling off to uncover the painting of the stretched canvas underneath. It's a trick to fool the eye, trompe l'oeil, a tradition in art history. To make the illusion convincing, an artist has to be masterful. Like Roy.

The theme of looking, or how people see, had long concerned him. As early as 1964 he had painted *Girl in Mirror*, a smiling blond gazing at herself in a hand mirror. This subject had been a favorite of artists in the past. Pablo Picasso, for instance, had depicted a woman looking at herself in a hand mirror (without seeing a reflection) in his painting *La coiffure*. And before him, in 1656, Diego Velázquez had painted *Las Meninas (The Maids of Honor)*, in which he cleverly included a mirror reflecting figures *outside* the painting.

In Roy's new series of Mirror paintings, started in 1969, what interested him was the play of light on and in the glass, and how to depict these shadowy effects. His enormous pictures, some as large as eight feet, are almost purely abstract patterns of dots, lines, and solid colors.

At that time his studio was in the Bowery in New York City. When he walked past neighborhood stores that sold glass and mirrors, he noticed printed catalogs in the windows. Back in his studio, he saw ads for mirrors in newspapers, catalogs, and the yellow pages. Roy liked the airbrushed shadows in the cheap commercial illustrations. Intrigued, he filled his sketchbooks with sensitive pencil drawings of various mirrors—round, oval, rectangular. He developed many of these into studies and completed about fifty elegant Mirror paintings. "My first mirror paintings didn't really look like mirrors to people," he said. They were

GIRL IN MIRROR, 1964.

too abstract. "It required a little learning to make them understandable as mirrors." However, collectors and museum curators came to love them.

In 1973 he developed a group of paintings based on fine art rather than comics or ads. "All my art is in some way about other art, even if the other art is cartoons," said Roy. "I'm taking work of the past and turning it into my own style. Everybody does that." As far back as the sixteenth century, artists had created original paintings modeled after, "quoting," or remixing the work of other artists. In the twentieth century, Picasso had done etchings and paintings based on everything from ancient Greek and Roman art to paintings by Velázquez. Now Roy was inspired by Henri Matisse.

He had come across reproductions of Matisse's paintings based on his workplace. In *The Red Studio*, Matisse had included some of his own paintings and sculptures. "The idea of an intimate, romantic interior of an artist's studio was something I was interested in commenting on," said Roy. So he painted *Artist's Studio No. 1 (Look Mickey)*, a cartoon rendition of *his* studio painted in *his* unique style. There's the Donald Duck part of his *Look Mickey* above the couch (based on a newspaper ad), a Stretcher Frame painting propped against the door, and a large Mirror painting hanging on the adjacent wall. A comic book painting with only a word balloon that Roy made up says: "**SEE** THAT BALDHEADED GUY OVER THERE? THAT'S 'CURLY' **GROGAN**. HE AND HIS MOB **RUN** HALF THE RACKETS IN THIS **TOWN**!" It was Roy's joke about one of his friends who constantly thought about gangsters. Roy used strong black outlines to define forms, such as the couch and lamp, rather than tones of contrasting colors as Matisse had done.

By the early 1970s Roy was a star in the art world. In 1969 he had his first retrospective of paintings and sculpture at the Guggenheim Museum in New York, and the show traveled to three other American museums. In Paris and London he attended festive openings of his shows at galleries. Seeing his paintings displayed in a different setting away from his studio gave him the chance, he said, "to stand back and think about what you've done a little bit."

Journalists and scholars wrote books, catalogs, and magazine articles about his work. Filmmakers did movies showing him painting. Photographers came to his studio and took pictures. Roy received awards and many honorary degrees. The prices for his art climbed higher and higher. Yet despite international acclaim, Roy felt that his popularity could vanish at any minute. "The work is so acceptable now," he remarked to a friend. "It is sort of amazing that people have taken to it this way." His wife Dorothy said, "It was fifteen or even twenty years into this success . . . [before] he began to believe all the articles and the PR [publicity]."

LEFT: ARTIST'S STUDIO NO. 1 (LOOK MICKEY), 1973.

OPPOSITE: THE RED STUDIO, 1911, BY HENRI MATISSE.

ROY POSES IN FRONT OF MURAL WITH
BLUE BRUSHSTROKE, 1985.

In 1971 Roy and his family bought a house in Southampton, Long Island, and he moved his studio there, leaving New York City for almost a dozen years. There, on the eastern end of Long Island, he could work seven days a week, six hours a day. Every morning began with exercise followed by breakfast. He went into the studio at ten A.M., took a break for lunch at one P.M., then returned to work until five P.M. "He works in a very orderly way, purposeful but unhurried," observed a photographer who had become Roy's friend.

Music filled the studio, from speakers mounted high on shelves above jars of paint. Roy especially loved jazz—Miles Davis, John Coltrane, Charlie Parker, Billie Holiday, Sonny Rollins.

In 1982 Roy reestablished a studio and residence in New York City. One of his most challenging projects came along in 1984, when he was sixty-one years old. The Equitable Life Assurance Society commissioned him to create a five-story-high mural for the atrium of its new tower building in Manhattan. Most public murals have serious themes. Roy, typical of his sense of humor, wanted to poke fun at such murals. "I tried to construct it the way I would if I were saying something important," he told an art critic. "It has no theme whatever, but it seems to be saying something."

The mural presents a summary of his own art and references to twentieth-century masters. There's his composition notebook, Swiss cheese, and a figure holding a beach ball (like Roy's *Girl with Ball*). He added other elements from his paintings—a stylized sunburst, a hand with a sponge jokingly wiping away the mural, and an enormous blue brushstroke. "This is going to be the world's biggest brushstroke," he said. "At times the brushstroke looks like a waterfall to me, but then it looks as if someone threw a pail of water out the window. That's why I call it MURAL WITH BLUE BRUSHSTROKE." (In the mural, the window lines up exactly with the building's window.) He wanted people to enjoy the mural and laugh or smile when they saw it. He said, "Early on I could see that some passersby immediately understood the humor of my work."

When he began drawing the composition, he included a comic book painting he had done in 1961 called *Knock Knock*. It shows a door like the one in the painting of his studio, with the words "Knock Knock" and "blast symbols" representing the sound. However, when members of the Assurance Society saw the preparatory color study, they objected to the cartoon words. Reluctantly, Roy left them out.

He developed the composition by making collages. "A collage tells me more exactly what the painting is going to be," he said. When the final collage was approved, Roy projected it from a tower he had built onto canvas that had been attached to the atrium wall. Drawing was done from a swing stage, and painting from scaffolding. He drew the outlines in pencil, then in black tape so that he could stand far back to study the design and make corrections. With the help of assistants, he painted the shapes, using eighteen colors instead of his usual four or five. The mural was finished in six weeks. At the unveiling, Roy perched on top of a tall ladder and posed for photos in front of the mural. His head only reached his signature in the bottom right-hand corner.

From this gigantic mural to small postcard-size sketches, Roy brought joy, thoughtfulness, and skill to his work. For him drawing was "fundamental to art." He said, "It's the first thing I do. It's a way of describing my thoughts as quickly as possible and then preparing to make a painting or larger drawing."

SUMMER MOUNTAINS, NORTH SONG DYNASTY HAND SCROLL, 1023–1056 C.E., ATTRIBUTED TO QU DING.

In 1987 the Museum of Modern Art in New York held a retrospective exhibition of Roy's drawings, and the show traveled to museums in the United States and Europe. During the following ten years, Roy kept drawing as he worked on a variety of projects: sculptures, prints, and paintings. He revisited old themes and turned to new ones.

He even started taking saxophone lessons and went upstairs to his living quarters, above the New York studio, to practice at the end of the day. His teacher, Hayes Greenfield, said that "Roy was a natural talent." Soon Roy played well enough to sit in with Greenfield's jazz band and perform with kids in an after-school program.

One of Roy's last art series in 1996 was a group of large horizontal and vertical paintings that he called Landscapes in the Chinese Style. The idea came to him when he saw a show of Edgar Degas's pastel landscapes at the Metropolitan Museum of Art. Roy said he was also inspired by the museum's Song Dynasty Chinese landscapes. As usual he began with sketches. Then he made collages with tape and painted and printed paper to plan his compositions. In the painting *Vista with Bridge* the blue and black Benday dots grow smaller and smaller and are spaced farther apart until they fade away into a light blue sky. The dots create the illusion of mountains receding into the distance. Compared to the grandeur of nature, people are very small. Looking closely one sees tiny figures crossing a bridge. Roy's modern painting captures the airiness and serenity of the ancient Chinese scrolls. The exquisite paintings were exhibited at the Leo Castelli Gallery and this was to be Roy's last show there.

He was in the middle of developing a new series of works when he became sick with pneumonia, developed a severe infection, and died on September 29, 1997, at the age of seventy-three. However, Roy's place was firmly established in the world of art. Over the years he had produced more than a thousand paintings, almost three thousand works on paper, about three hundred sculptures, and fifty-eight ceramics. Yet throughout his career Roy had pondered the same old question: "Who's to say it's art and who's to say it's good and who's to say it should be there?"

Critic Roberta Smith said it best: Roy's "tender" drawings and "the perfection of his paintings" reveal "his rapt devotion to his art."

Wow!

Whaam!

VISTA WITH BRIDGE, 1996.

Glossary

Abstract Expressionist: An artist who did not represent anything recognizable in his or her work but created paintings with color and line to express emotion and appreciation of paint for its own sake. The art movement Abstract Expressionism, developed after World War II.

Abstraction: A painting in which the subject is not something recognizable, but a composition of shapes, lines, and/or patterns from the artist's imagination.

Cartoon: A sketch or drawing, usually humorous, that exaggerates a person or an action.

Cast: To form an object by pouring plaster or melted metal into a mold and letting it harden. Also an object made by this method.

Cézanne, Paul: A French painter (1839–1906) whose work linked late-nineteenth-century Impressionism with the radically different art of the twentieth century. His work demonstrates a mastery of design, color, composition, and draftsmanship.

Cliché: A word, thought, or image that is overused to the point that it loses its intended force or novelty.

Collage: An artwork created by pasting pieces of paper, fabric, photographs, or other materials onto a single surface.

Comics and comic strip: Comics (comic books) are a popular form of storytelling through illustrations and words (often in word bubbles or captions). A comic strip is a panel of pictures with or without words that usually appears in newspapers and magazines.

Composition: The arrangement or organization of shapes and lines on a two-dimensional surface.

Critic: A person who judges and evaluates an artistic work.

Curator: A person who organizes a museum art collection and/or exhibit.

Dealer: The owner of an art gallery who exhibits and sells an artist's work.

Fabricator: A skilled craftsperson who assembles or constructs a work of art.

Fine art: Works of art that meet standards of beauty agreed upon by museums without regard to sales and public opinion.

Flat color: A color (painted or printed) that is smooth and even without shading or brush marks.

Foundry: A place for producing casts in melted metal.

Gallery: A room or building devoted to exhibiting art.

Illustration: A picture that explains, clarifies, or decorates text.

Klee, Paul: A Swiss painter (1879–1940) of German nationality who was influenced by many different art styles, including Surrealism, and used symbols, letters, and numbers to portray his dreams, fantasies, and musical feelings.

Landscape: A painting based on nature in which scenery is the main subject.

Mark: A line, stroke, smear, or shape on a surface.

Mass-produce: To manufacture items identically in large quantities by machinery.

Mural: A large picture painted directly on a wall or attached to it.

Perceptual unit: An image or object that is seen as a whole and not broken up into parts.

Picasso, Pablo: A Spanish painter (1881–1973) and sculptor and one of the most recognized figures in twentieth-century art, best known as the cofounder, along with Georges Braque, of Cubism.

Pop Art: Art that features images taken from popular culture.

Portrait: A painting or drawing of a person or animal that captures a physical likeness or reveals character and inner spirit.

Proportion: The relative size of one thing to another, such as a part to the whole.

Reproduction: A printed copy of an original image or object.

Retrospective: An art exhibit that showcases an entire period of an artist's work.

Scale model, or maquette: A small preliminary representation of an artwork constructed in the same proportions as the larger, final piece.

Sculpture: A three-dimensional artwork.

Self-portrait: A picture that an artist paints, draws, or photographs of himself or herself.

Silk screen: A mesh stencil used for color printing, or a work made with such a stencil.

Sketch: A drawing done quickly and loosely without details.

Studio: The workroom of an artist.

Stylized: A repeated, symbolic way of representing an image.

Subject: An object, scene, pattern, or motif that an artist chooses to represent.

Theme: A unifying idea in a work of art.

Three-dimensional: A work of art that has depth as well as width and height and occupies real space.

Two-dimensional: A work of art on a flat surface, such as paper or canvas, that has only height and width.

Notes

Page 3: "And you're an . . . can't draw." Chuck Csuri to Avis Berman, quoted in "The Transformation of Roy Lichtenstein: An Oral History," *Roy Lichtenstein: All About Art*, eds. Michael Juul Holm, Poul Erik Tøjner, and Martin Caiger-Smith (Denmark: The Louisiana Museum of Modern Art, 2003), p. 124.

Page 3: "When I put . . . to the abstractions." Roy Lichtenstein to Lawrence Alloway in video *Lichtenstein, Part 1 and 2* (Blackwood Productions, 1976).

Page 4: "His friends . . . him paint." Mrs. Renée Tolcott to author, February 7, 2007.

Page 6: "He explained . . . to me." Ibid.

Page 6: "I was . . . swimming." Roy Lichtenstein to Calvin Tomkins in *Roy Lichtenstein: Mural with Blue Brushstroke* (New York: Harry N. Abrams, 1988), p. 13.

Page 6: "His projects . . . schoolwork." Mrs. Renée Tolcott to author, February 7, 2007.

Page 8: "I had no . . . the whole thing." Roy Lichtenstein quoted in Tomkins, *Mural with Blue Brushstroke*, p. 14.

Page 8: "He taught . . . to look." Roy Lichtenstein quoted in Bonnie Clearwater, *Roy Lichtenstein: Inside/Outside*, (North Miami: Museum of Contemporary Art, 2001), p. 115.

Page 8: "flash labs." Jack Cowart to author, November 15, 2006.

Page 8: "The images . . . more complex." Roy Lichtenstein quoted in Bonnie Clearwater, *Roy Lichtenstein: Inside/Outside*, p. 18.

Page 8: "If a person . . . perceptual unit." Hoyt Sherman quoted in ibid., p. 32.

Page 8: "became the center . . . one that wasn't." Roy Lichtenstein quoted in Tomkins, *Mural with Blue Brushstroke*, p. 15.

Page 9: "We were . . . at that point." Ibid., p. 15.

Page 9: "In awe . . . electric expression." Roy Lichtenstein quoted in "Paintings, Drawings and Pastels: A Thesis by Roy Fox Lichtenstein, 1949," Mitchell-Innes and Nash, *Roy Lichtenstein: Conversations with Surrealism* (New York: Roy Lichtenstein Foundation, 2005), p. 3.

Page 10: "I was painting . . . modern way. " Roy Lichtenstein quoted in Tomkins, *Mural with Blue Brushstroke*, p. 16.

Page 12: "I began . . . Bugs Bunny." Roy Lichtenstein quoted in Bruce Glaser, *Lichtenstein: Sculptures and Drawings* (Corcoran Gallery of Art and Roy Lichtenstein Foundation, 1998 and 1999), p. 41.

Page 13: "the greatest influence . . . said before." Roy Lichtenstein quoted in Tomkins, *Mural with Blue Brushstroke*, p. 20.

Page 13: "create fresh, new designs." Hoyt Sherman quoted in Hoyt Sherman, *A Manual Operation with an Emphasis on the Arts: The Visual Demonstration Center*, Part 1 (Columbus, Ohio: Ohio State University, 1951).

Pages 13–15: "You can't teach . . . Duck in it." Allan Kaprow quoted in Tomkins, *Mural with Blue Brushstroke*, p. 21.

Page 15: "I got . . . one another." Roy Lichtenstein to Diane Waldman, *Roy Lichtenstein* (New York: Abrams, 1971), p. 26.

Page 15: "I'm not using . . . commercial techniques." Roy Lichtenstein in video *Lichtenstein, Part 1 and 2* (Blackwood Productions, 1976).

Pages 16–18: "What I did . . . really appreciated . . . no humanity . . . done before." Ibid.

Page 19: "possibilities for paintings." Roy Lichtenstein quoted in Bradford R. Collins, "Modern Romance: Lichtenstein's Comic Book Paintings," *American Art 17, no. 2* (Summer 2003), p. 61.

Page 19: "non-art." Roy Lichtenstein quoted in Dorothy Seiberling "Is He the Worse Artist in the U.S.?" *Life*, January 31, 1964.

Page 20: "Food always . . . in Pop." Roy Lichtenstein in video *Lichtenstein, Part 1 and 2* (Blackwood Productions, 1976).

Page 20: "I am annoyed . . . in a supermarket." Barbara Rose quoted in "Pop Art at the Guggenheim," *Art International*, May 1963, in *Pop Art: A Critical History*, ed. Steven Henry Madoff, (Berkeley: University of California Press, 1997), p. 82.

Page 20: "apprehensive." Roy Lichtenstein in video *Lichtenstein, Part 1 and 2* (Blackwood Productions, 1976).

Pages 20: "My work . . . nothing is the same." Roy Lichtenstein to John Coplans, ibid.

Page 21: "jokey" and "empty-headed." Christopher Knight, *New York Times*, September 30, 1997.

Page 21: "Pop Artists or Copy Cats?" Erle Loran, *Art News*, September 1963.

Page 21: "one of . . . in the world." Peter Benchley quoting *New York Times* critic in Madoff, *Pop Art: A Critical History*, p. 149.

Pages 21: "Is he . . . but is it art?" Seiberling, "Is He the Worst Artist in the U.S.?" *Life*, January 31, 1964, pp. 79–83.

Page 24: "I had always . . , one that wasn't." Roy Lichtenstein quoted in Tomkins, *Mural with Blue Brushstroke*, p. 15.

Page 24: "This is art." Roy Lichtenstein to Diane Waldman, *Roy Lichtenstein* (Abrams, 1971), p. 28.

Page 25: "My dream . . . can't believe it." Roy Lichtenstein to Sidney Chafetz, quoted in Avis Berman, "The Transformations of Roy Lichtenstein: An Oral History," *Roy Lichtenstein: All About Art*, eds. Holm, Tøjner, and Caiger-Smith, p. 132.

Page 25: "I wonder . . . going to last." Roy Lichtenstein to Bruce Beland, ibid., p. 133.

Page 27: "Very flattering . . . I think?" William Overgard, *Time*, August 6, 1961.

Page 28: "I really think . . . other shape." Roy Lichtenstein to Diane Waldman, *Roy Lichtenstein* (Abrams, 1971), p. 28.

Page 28: "Most of my . . . as much as possible." Roy Lichtenstein to Lawrence Alloway in video *Lichtenstein, Part 1 and 2* (Blackwood Productions, 1976).

Page 28: "Once I am . . . when I work." Roy Lichtenstein quoted in Janis Hendrickson, *Lichtenstein* (Bonn, Germany: Taschen 2001), p. 45.

Page 28: "When you suddenly . . . first time." Roy Lichtenstein to Lawrence Alloway in video *Lichtenstein, Part 1 and 2* (Blackwood Productions, 1976).

Page 30: "I did . . . at that time." Roy Lichtenstein to Diane Waldman, *Roy Lichtenstein* (Abrams, 1971), p. 27.

Page 32: "I've always wanted . . . a three-dimensional object." Roy Lichtenstein to John Coplans in *Roy Lichtenstein* (Pasadena Art Museum/Walker Art Center/Pop Art USA, catalog, Oakland Art Museum, 1963), p. 16.

Page 32: "The starting point . . . comic book." Roy Lichtenstein in video *Roy Lichtenstein: Tokyo Brushstrokes* (New York: Checkerboard Productions, 1995).

Page 33: "Although I had played . . . artist's hand." Roy Lichtenstein to John Coplans, *Roy Lichtenstein* (Pasadena Art Museum/Walker Art Center/Pop Art USA), p. 15.

Page 33: "I must be . . . kind of nightmare." Dick Giordano, panel from "The Painting" in *Strange Suspense Stories*, no. 72 (October 1964).

Page 33: "The brush strokes . . . Abstract Expressionism." Roy Lichtenstein to John Coplans in *Roy Lichtenstein* (Pasadena Art Museum/Walker Art Center/Pop Art USA, catalog, Oakland Art Museum, 1963), p. 15.

Page 33: "I thought . . . like bacon or something." Roy Lichtenstein in video *Tokyo Brushstrokes* (Checkerboard Productions, 1995).

Page 33: "It was just . . . a certain way." Roy Lichtenstein, ibid.

Page 34: "I think . . . around it." Roy Lichtenstein, ibid.

Page 34: "I felt victorious . . . sort of amazing!" Roy Lichtenstein, ibid.

Page 35: "something . . . haven't seen." Roy Lichtenstein, quoted in Clearwater, *Roy Lichtenstein: Inside/Outside*, p. 15.

Page 36–38: "My first mirror . . . as mirrors." Roy Lichtenstein quoted in Diane Waldman, *Roy Lichtenstein* (New York: Guggenheim Museum, 1994), p. 183.

Page 38: "All my art . . . is cartoons." Roy Lichtenstein in Tomkins, *Mural with Blue Brushstroke*, p. 122.

Page 38: "I'm taking . . . does that." Roy Lichtenstein in video *The Drawings of Roy Lichtenstein*, 1961–1986 (New York: Checkerboard Foundation, 1987).

Page 38: "The idea of . . . commenting on." Roy Lichtenstein, ibid.

Page 39: "to stand back . . . a little bit." Roy Lichtenstein in video *Lichtenstein, Part 1 and 2* (Blackwood Productions, 1976).

Page 39: "The work is . . . this way." Roy Lichtenstein to Calvin Tomkins, *Mural with Blue Brushstroke*, p. 13.

Page 39: "It was fifteen . . . and the PR [publicity]." Dorothy Lichtenstein to Avis Berman in "Roy Lichtenstein: An Oral History" *All About Art*, ed. Holm, Tøjner, and Caiger-Smith, p. 133.

Page 40: "He works . . . but unhurried." Bob Adelman in Tomkins, *Mural with a Blue Brushstroke*, p. 36.

Page 40: "I tried to construct . . . saying something." Roy Lichtenstein to Calvin Tomkins, *Mural with a Blue Brushstroke*, p. 10.

Page 41: "This is . . . biggest brushstroke." Roy Lichtenstein to Bob Adelman in ibid., p. 58.

Page 41: "At times . . . BLUE BRUSHSTROKE." Ibid., p. 123.

Page 41: "Early on . . . my work." Ibid., p. 99.

Page 41: "A collage . . . going to be." Ibid., p. 50.

Page 41: "fundamental to art . . . It's the . . . or larger drawing." Roy Lichtenstein to Bernice Rose in video *The Drawings of Roy Lichtenstein, 1961–1986* for exhibit at Museum of Modern Art, New York.

Page 42: "Roy was a natural talent." Hayes Greenfield to the author, January 18, 2007.

Page 43: "Who's to say . . . should be there?" Roy Lichtenstein in video *Tokyo Brushstrokes* (Checkerboard Productions, 1995).

Page 43: "tender," "the perfection . . . his paintings," "his rapt . . . to his art." Roberta Smith, "Roy Lichtenstein," Art in Review, *New York Times*, January 12, 2007, p. B40.

References & Resources

* Denotes material suitable for younger readers

Books

*Adelman, Bob. *Roy Lichtenstein's ABC*. Boston and New York: Little, Brown and Company, 1999.

Alloway, Lawrence. *Lichtenstein*. New York: Abbeville Press, 1983.

*Boris, Janet. *Roy Lichtenstein: Art Ed Books and Kit*. New York: Abrams, 2001.

Corlett, Mary Lee. *The Prints of Roy Lichtenstein: A Catalogue Raisonné 1948–1997*. New York: Hudson Hills Press in Association with the National Gallery of Art, Washington, D.C., 2002.

Cowart, Jack. *Lichtenstein: Sculpture and Drawings*. Washington, D.C.: Corcoran Gallery of Art, 1999.

Hendrickson, Janis. *Lichtenstein*. Bonn, Germany: Taschen, 2001.

Holm, Michael Juul, Poul Erik Tøjner, and Martin Caiger-Smith, eds. *Roy Lichtenstein: All About Art*. Denmark: Louisiana Museum of Modern Art, Denmark, 2003.

Madoff, Steven Henry, ed. *Pop Art: A Critical History*. Berkeley: University of California Press, 1997.

Schneider, Eckhard, ed. *Roy Lichtenstein: Classic of the New*. Cologne, Germany: Kunsthaus Bregenz, 2005.

Sherman, Hoyt. *A Manual of Operation with an Emphasis on the Arts: The Visual Demonstration Center*, part 1. Columbus, Ohio: Ohio State University, 1951.

Stavitsky, Gail, and Twig Johnson. *Roy Lichtenstein: American Indian Encounters*. Montclair, New Jersey: Montclair Art Museum, 2005.

Tomkins, Calvin, and photographs with interview by Bob Adelman. *Roy Lichtenstein: Mural with Blue Brushstroke*. New York: Harry N. Abrams, 1988.

Varnedoe, Kirk, and Adam Gopnik. *High and Low: Modern Art, Popular Culture*. New York: Museum of Modern Art, 1991.

*Venezia, Mike. *Roy Lichtenstein*. New York: Children's Press, 2001.

Waldman, Diane. *Roy Lichtenstein*. New York: Guggenheim Museum, 1993.

———. *Roy Lichtenstein*. New York: Abrams, 1971.

*Walker, Lou Ann. *Roy Lichtenstein: The Artist at Work*. New York: Dutton/Lodestar, 1994.

Exhibition Catalogs

Bois, Yves-Alain. *Roy Lichtenstein: Perfect/Imperfect*. Beverly Hills, California: Gagosian Gallery, 2002.

Clearwater, Bonnie. *Roy Lichtenstein: Inside/Outside*. North Miami: Museum of Contemporary Art, 2001.

Coplans, John. *Roy Lichtenstein. Pop Art USA*. Oakland Art Museum, 1963.

Dibujos. *Roy Lichtenstein: Animated Life*. São Paulo, Brazil: Instituto Tomie Ohtake, 2005; and New York: Solomon R. Guggenheim Museum, 1993 and 1998.

Lichtenstein: en proceso. Cuenca, Spain: Museo de Arte Abstracto Español, 2005.

Lichtenstein, Roy. *Landscapes in Chinese Style*. Hong Kong: Hong Kong Museum of Fine Art, 1998.

Mitchell-Innes and Nash. *Roy Lichtenstein: Conversations with Surrealism*. New York: Roy Lichtenstein Foundation, 2005.

Rose, Bernice. *The Drawings of Roy Lichtenstein.* New York: The Museum of Modern Art, 1987.

Roy Lichtenstein Prints 1956–97. Washington State University/ Museum of Art, 2005.

Roy Lichtenstein Sculpture. New York and London: Gagosian Gallery, 2005.

Articles

Baker, Elizabeth C. "Riding Horses on the Beach, Talking Art in a Loft." *New York Times*, October 5, 1997.

Collins, Bradford R. "Modern Romance: Lichtenstein's Comic Book Paintings." *American Art 17*, no. 2 (Summer 2003).

Felsen, Sidney B. "A Pop Icon Is Remembered for His Humor and Kindness." *Los Angeles Times*, October 1, 1997.

Knight, Christopher. "Pop Art Icon Lichtenstein Dies." *Los Angeles Times*, September 30, 1997.

Loran, Erle. "Pop Artists or Copy Cats?" *Art News*, September 1963.

Seiberling, Dorothy. "Is He the Worst Artist in the U.S.?" *Life*, January 31, 1964.

Smith, Roberta. "Roy Lichtenstein." Art in Review. *New York Times*, January 12, 2007.

Swenson, G. R. *Roy Lichtenstein: An Interview.* Tate Gallery, January 6–February 4, 1968.

Videos

Lichtenstein, Part 1 and 2. Directed by Michael Blackwood, consultant Diane Waldman, produced by Blackwood Productions for Telefilm Saar and RM Productions, 1976.

Roy Lichtenstein: Tokyo Brushstrokes. New York, produced by Edgar B. Howard, directed by Mark Trottenberg, with original music by Hayes Greenfield, curated by Fumio Najo, and produced by Edgar B. Howard. New York: Checkerboard Productions, 1995.

Roy Lichtenstein: Reflections. Checkerboard Foundation.

The Drawings of Roy Lichtenstein, 1961–1986. Produced in association with the Museum of Modern Art. New York: Checkerboard Foundation, Inc., 1987.

USA: Artists—Warhol and Lichtenstein.

Remembering Roy Lichtenstein. Montclair Art Museum, Nineteenth Annual Julia Norton Babson Memorial Lecture, November 6, 2005.

Roy Lichtenstein in the Tel Aviv Museum of Art. Directed by Tami Eyal, produced by the Tel Aviv Museum of Art and Camera Obscura School of Art.

CDs

*Jazz-A-Ma-Tazz, Hayes Greenfield. Produced by Hayes Greenfield, executive producers Roy and Dorothy Lichtenstein. Liquid Records and Entertainment, 1998.

*The Melody Haunts My Reverie . . . The Music of Roy Lichtenstein. Hayes Greenfield, Shelley Lee, and Dorothy Lichtenstein. Universal Music, Austria, 2003.

Interviews conducted by the author

Hayes Greenfield, January 18, 2007

Mrs. Renée Tolcott, over the phone, February 7, 2007, and February 10, 2007.

Museums & Public Places Where You Will Find Work by Roy Lichtenstein

In the United States

Art Institute of Chicago, Illinois

AXA Equitable Building, 787 Seventh Avenue, New York City

Denver Art Museum, Colorado

Des Moines Art Center, Iowa

Hirshhorn Museum and Sculpture Garden, Washington, D.C.

Milwaukee Art Museum, Wisconsin

Modern Art Museum of Fort Worth, Texas

Museum of Contemporary Art, Los Angeles, California

Museum of Modern Art, New York City

National Gallery of Art, Washington, D.C.

Nelson-Atkins Museum, Kansas City, Missouri

Port Columbus International Airport, Columbus, Ohio

San Francisco Museum of Modern Art, California

St. Louis Art Museum, Missouri

Whitney Museum of American Art, New York City

Yale University Art Gallery, New Haven, Connecticut

Outside the United States

Israel Museum, Jerusalem, Israel

Ludwig Forum für Internationale Kunst, Aachen, Germany

Museum Ludwig, Cologne, Germany

Osaka Maritime Museum, Osaka, Japan

Tate Gallery, London, England

Tel Aviv Museum of Art, Tel Aviv, Israel

Acknowledgments

I am deeply grateful to the Roy Lichtenstein Foundation for allowing me to have the joyful experience of researching in Roy's studio, surrounded by his art. I thank Dorothy Lichtenstein, Jack Cowart, Shelley Lee, Cassandra Lozano, Clare Bell, Natasha Sigmund, and Angela Ferguson for their cooperation and assistance.

My thanks to Mrs. Renée Tolcott for talking with me over the phone and telling me about growing up with her brother, Roy. I also want to thank Roy's saxophone teacher and friend Hayes Greenfield for meeting with me.

At Abrams I thank my editor, Howard Reeves, for the skill, taste, and dedication that he brings to producing art books for young readers. It is a pleasure to work with him. Special thanks to Maria Middleton, and to Chad Beckerman, art director, for designing the book; Jason Wells, marketing director; and Maggie Lehrman, assistant editor. As always, I owe a debt of gratitude to George Nicholson for his enthusiasm, encouragement, and guidance, and I thank his assistants past and present, Emily Hazel and Victoria Marini. I especially appreciate the critiques from my friends in Lunch Bunch and the Thursday night group. And, of course, I extend my heartfelt thanks to my husband, Michael.

Illustration Credits

Index

FOR MY COUSIN NANCY COGGAN KOHN

Library of Congress Cataloging-in-Publication Data

Rubin, Susan Goldman.
Whaam! : the art and life of Roy Lichtenstein / by Susan Goldman Rubin.
p. cm.
ISBN 978-0-8109-9492-8
1. Lichtenstein, Roy, 1923–1997—Juvenile literature. 2. Artists—United States—Biography—Juvenile literature.
3. Pop art—United States—Juvenile literature. I. Title.

N6537.L5R83 2008
709.2—dc22
[B]
2007042048

Book design by Maria T. Middleton

Text copyright © 2008 Susan Goldman Rubin

For illustration credits, please see page 46.

Printed and bound in China
10 9 8 7 6 5 4 3 2 1

HNA
harry n. abrams, inc.
a subsidiary of La Martinière Groupe

115 West 18th Street
New York, NY 10011
www.hnabooks.com